MCL

HORSEPOWER

TUNER CARS

by Sarah L. Schuette

Reading Consultant:

Barbara J. Fox

Reading Specialist

North Carolina State University

Capstone
press

Mankato, Minnesota

Blazers is published by Capstone Press,
151 Good Counsel Drive, P.O. Box 669, Mankato, Minnesota 56002.
www.capstonepress.com

Library of Congress Cataloging-in-Publication Data
Schuette, Sarah L., 1976–
Tuner cars / by Sarah L. Schuette.
    p. cm.—(Blazers. Horsepower)
    Summary: "Describes tuner cars, their main features, and how
they are raced"—Provided by publisher.
    Includes bibliographical references and index.
    ISBN-13: 978-0-7368-5475-7 (hardcover)
    ISBN-10: 0-7368-5475-4 (hardcover)
    1. Hot rods—Juvenile literature. 2. Automobiles
Performance—Juvenile literature. I. Title. II. Series.
TL236.3.S34 2006
629.228'6—dc22   2005026184

Editorial Credits

Mandy Marx, editor; Jason Knudson, set designer; Thomas Emery,
    book designer; Jo Miller, photo researcher; Scott Thoms,
    photo editor

Photo Credits

Artemis Images, 12, 13, 14, 15, 25
Getty Images Inc./Ker Robertson, 26–27
Grand American Road Racing/Brian Cleary, 5, 6, 7, 8–9
Mercury Press International/Isaac Hernandez, 20–21
Ron Kimball Stock, cover; Ron Kimball, 11, 16–17, 19 (both),
    20, 21, 22, 28–29

The author dedicates this book to her Uncle Jon Schuette of Belle
Plaine Auto, Belle Plaine, Minnesota.

1 2 3 4 5 6 11 10 09 08 07 06

TABLE OF CONTENTS

ON THE TRACK

A tuned-up Nissan thunders down the track. The driver downshifts. He stomps on the gas pedal.

The Nissan easily pulls ahead
of the pack. It hugs the curves.
The other cars can't catch up.

Tuner cars compete in Grand American Road Racing Association events. Tuners reach speeds of about 135 miles (217 kilometers) per hour in these events.

Cruising across the finish line, this tuner car is the fastest of the group. Soon, it will race other tuners for top honors.

Racing tuner cars on the street is illegal. Cars can only race on a track.

TUNER DESIGN

Many tuner cars are made in Japan or Europe. Tuner cars are small, but they are more powerful than the average car.

A turbocharger boosts power to the engine. Turbocharged engines give tuners a quick start.

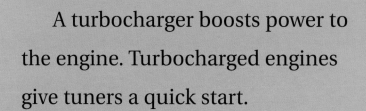

BLAZER FACT

The Nissan Skyline is one of the most popular tuner cars.

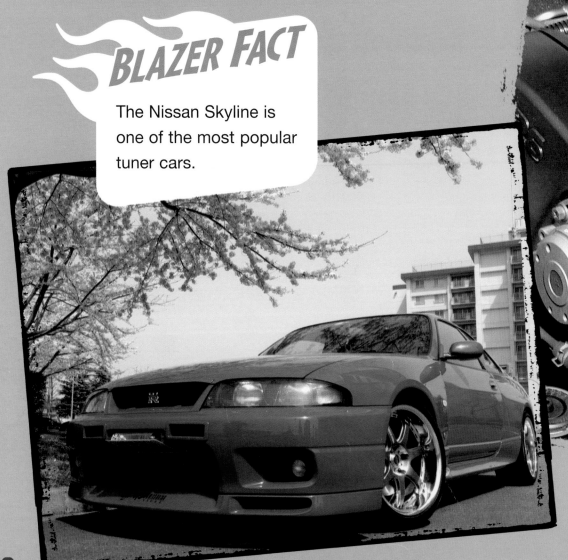

Gauges

Drivers keep a close eye on their gauges. Gauges let drivers know when to shift. They also alert drivers if the engine is getting too hot.

BLAZER FACT

Air intakes bring more air into the engine. The extra air helps the engine produce more horsepower.

Air intake

TUNER CAR DIAGRAM

Bumper cover

Flashy paint job

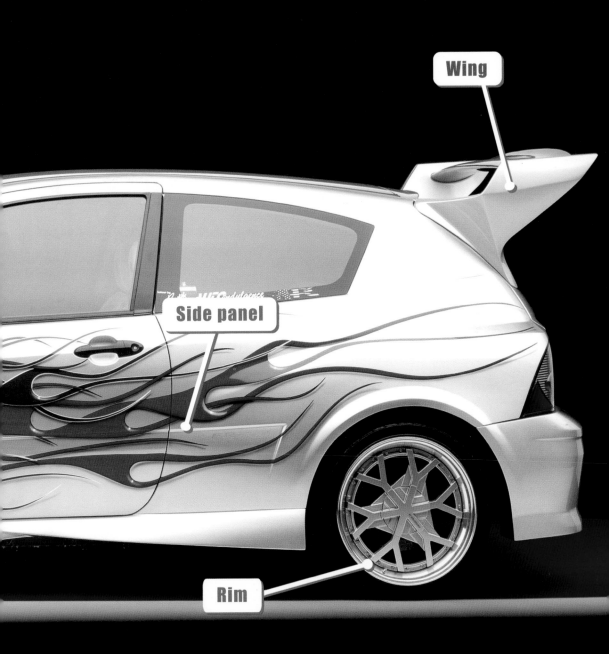

Wing

Side panel

Rim

TUNER STYLE

Boosting power is only half of tuning up a car. Flashy paint, shiny rims, and added body panels give them style.

Factory model Honda Civic

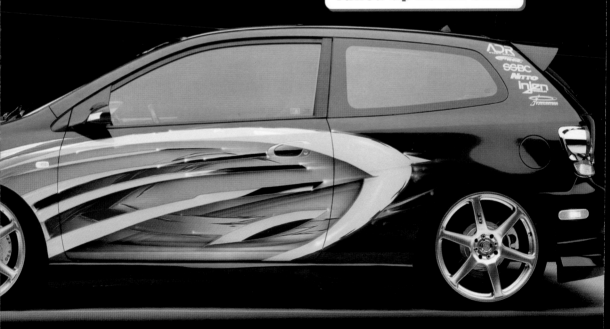

Tuned-up Honda Civic

New lambo doors

Tuning is a complete car makeover. New doors, bumper covers, and wings create a hot new look.

Bumper cover

Wing

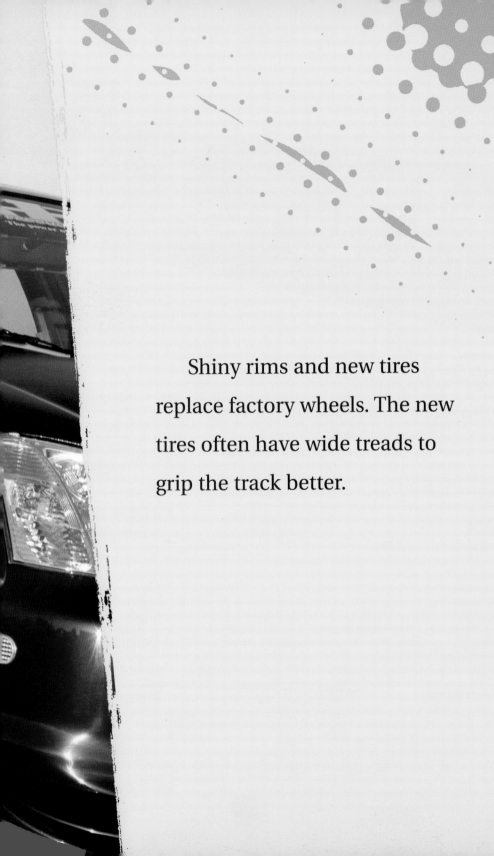

Shiny rims and new tires replace factory wheels. The new tires often have wide treads to grip the track better.

TUNERS
IN ACTION

In drifting races, drivers powerslide around turns. Tires screech. Cars sway back and forth, trying to pass each other.

Fans love to watch drifting and other tuner racing events. Engines roar as these high-powered cars whip around the track.

BLAZER FACT

The sport of drifting
began in Japan and
is now popular in the
United States.

TUNED TO
PERFECTION!

GLOSSARY

factory (FAK-tuh-ree)—the place where a product, such as a car, is made; the same basic model is made in mass quantities.

horsepower (HORSS-pou-ur)—a unit for measuring an engine's power

powerslide (POU-ur-slyde)—a sideways slide that the driver can control

rim (RIM)—the metal part of the wheel on which the tire is mounted

shift (SHIFT)—to change gears

treads (TREDS)—the ridges on a tire

turbocharged engine (TUR-boh-charjed EN-juhn)—an engine that has high-pressure air forced through it to produce extra power

READ MORE

Canter, Jay. *Tuner Cars Field Guide: Furiously Fast Sport Compacts.* Iola, Wis.: KP Books, 2005.

Doeden, Matt. *Dragsters.* Horsepower. Mankato, Minn.: Capstone Press, 2005.

Paradise, Alan. *Sport Compacts.* Enthusiast Color. St. Paul, Minn.: MBI, 2003.

INTERNET SITES

FactHound offers a safe, fun way to find Internet sites related to this book. All of the sites on FactHound have been researched by our staff.

Here's how:

1. Visit *www.facthound.com*
2. Type in this special code **0736854754** for age-appropriate sites. Or enter a search word related to this book for a more general search.
3. Click on the **Fetch It** button.

FactHound will fetch the best sites for you!

INDEX